You Are gOD

The 3 Core Powers of Success

Sean Taylor

Special discounts on bulk quantities of this book are available to corporations, professional associations, and other organizations. For details, email youaregodinfo@gmail.com.

Book website and author blog: **youaregodinfo.com**

You Are God: The 3 Core Powers of Success Copyright © 2014 Wurvo, LLC.

ISBN-13: 978-0692215463
ISBN-10: 0692215468

Publisher's Note

This publication is designed to provide accurate and authoritative information in regard to the subject matter covered. It is sold with the understanding that the publisher is not engaged in rendering legal, accounting, or other professional services. If you require legal advice or other expert assistance, you should seek the services of a competent professional.

Cover Design: Isaiah Brown, Sean Taylor
Editors: Bridgette Davis, Bob Land

Dad,
Thank you for all of the conversations.
Sometimes I spoke. Sometimes *we* spoke.
You *always* listened.

Uncle Mark,
I only have one vivid memory of you…
I was four years old.
It changed my life.
Thank you.

Mom,
You tested me before the world did.
My mind is strong because of it.
You forged my spirit.
You bolstered my resolve.
Above all,
You supported me
without understanding me.
Sometimes it hurt.
That is love.

Contents

The 4 Mindsets of Achievement

Core 3   Habit

Core Reinforcement: Keep This in Mind

Every day comes a new beginning

This is mine

Let today be yours

Forward

If decisions are easy to make, why is every person who attends a moneymaking seminar not rich? Why do people practice religion for years and still remain so far from where they desire to be? Why do we make New Year's resolutions only to revert to our old ways before the end of February? We know what to do, so all we have to do is do it, right?

Through dealing with ourselves and others over our lifetimes, we all learn that, ultimately, no one can really *make* anyone change. If someone does not choose to change, they simply will not. Notice this was not worded, "If someone does not *want* to change, they simply will not." Everyone has experienced *wanting* to change something about themselves and failing miserably, whether it is less procrastination, learning a new language, spending more time with family, becoming more spiritual, or quitting drinking and smoking. The list goes on and on.

Every now and then, "wanting" inspires "trying," but the sudden burst of energy lacks the persistence necessary to create a lasting result. The truth is that lasting change is not a result of a shot of inspiration. It takes consistent effort that can only be attained by a change in *thought process* and ultimately *habits*. In order to accomplish this, a decision must first be made.

With that said, a profound difference exists between desire and decision. Simply put, it is the juxtaposition of *What you want* vs. *What you won't do without*. When you want something, there is nothing else to it. You want "it," whatever "it" may be. When you will not do without something, then you instinctively do whatever you must to have it. At this point you make a true decision, a commitment to a new standard.

"A standard is not something that you "go" for. . . . It's not a goal. . . . It's something you LIVE, BREATHE, and find a way to get to, no matter what." —*Tony Robbins*

My goal for writing this book is simply to get this message out as clearly and concisely as possible, offering examples and interrelating concepts along the way for reinforcement. I hope this book acts as a catalyst for conversation and an impetus for epiphany. Even more, I hope to evoke new thoughts and initiate someone's *aha!* moment in their journey to the life they desire.

Ideally, when the dust settles, these ideas will at least be in your consideration as you go through life. The power does not necessarily lie in completely buying into an idea but merely in considering an idea or perception. Within additional perception lies growth and wisdom. This book does not simply describe then prescribe how to reach personal success, because everybody is different. Instead I offer basic but vital concepts that have the power to change your life if you commit to them.

"A man's mind, once stretched by a new idea, never regains its original dimensions." —*Oliver Wendell Holmes*

Why "You Are gOD"?

Whether your beliefs extend no further than the sciences or you believe in a higher power, we can all generally agree upon some things. We do not set our own lives into motion. Also, up until a certain age we do not have the capacity to adequately think or guide ourselves through life. This is the first phase of life, beginning at conception and lasting through childhood. During this phase, the catalysts that set us into motion and guide us through adolescence are God (if that is your belief), our parents, and other facets of our environment.

After the first phase, the world around us is largely the result of choices we make as individuals. We as human beings have great power in our ability to mold and remake our world. Gifted with conscious thought, we are all little creators, bringing our thoughts to life.

To be clear, using a lowercase *g* and uppercase *OD* for the word "god" simply provides a visual. The last two letters are capitalized to signify the aforementioned distribution of power as we come into our own. The *g* represents the first phase over which we have little to no control. The *O* represents the second phase where we first assume full responsibility for our actions and become the key determinant of our own lives. Finally, *D* is the third phase where our level of self-accountability allows us to build on the second phase and continue to dictate the lifestyle we lead.

"For every action, there is an equal and opposite reaction"; "You reap what you sow"; karma; "What goes around, comes around"—science, religions, and other ideals all acknowledge that our *choices* not only influence but determine outcome. Additionally, many successful people admit their talent to be nothing extraordinary and proudly pronounce their *mindset* as their reason for great achievement. It has also been proven that *habits*

are the most consistent—and often overlooked—factors that quietly determine success or failure.

Choice provides a compass, proper mindset helps weather the inevitable storms, and good habits ensure consistent progression. These are the 3 Core Powers of Success. These are the three fundamentals that allow us to tap into our potential and achieve great heights.

The 3 Core Powers of Success are effective separately and are even more powerful when used together. Still, for whatever reason, many people choose not to make great use of them. When a person actually exercises them to their full potential, onlookers often perceive the user to have something far more complex going on in life. Some even jokingly say the person is godlike, and in a sense that person is. . . . We all are. We all create. It is in our DNA. We are gODs.

If you by chance find
something worthwhile in
these pages - share it.
Information is one of the
most powerful gifts of all.

*"It is what you read when you don't have to that determines
what you will be when you can't help it."*
— Oscar Wilde

Core 1

Pure Choice

~ CHAPTER 1 ~

Making a Choice

We all want to live the best lives we can. We all have goals and search for the best ways to achieve them. Many people turn to books, seminars, and other sources. Whether the sources are people who have learned through experience or a group of researchers, they all suggest methods to help empower people through their own madness.

Unfortunately, these recommendations are all irrelevant without the mandatory catalyst. At the center of it all is a key element: *choice*. Whatever life you desire to lead, *this* is where it all begins. The problem is that making a choice seems so obvious, people often give this small detail *too little* attention.

When speaking of choice, I am particularly referring to a concept of choice in its purest form, uninterrupted by the noise of the many influences that cause individuals to waver in the tenacity with which they approach a task. To really decide, to truly make a choice, is certainly a phenomenon of its own. For the sake of this text, I refer to this phenomenon as Pure Choice.

Pure Choice is power. Pure Choice is finding out what we want *beyond* what other people want for us. We must not be limited by society's suggestions, internal doubts or immediate circumstances. Otherwise we will never realize our potential. It is not until we are able to sift through and quiet the noise that we can make a Pure Choice. When we do, we achieve a level of focus that allows us to accomplish things we never could have imagined. When we choose purely we can accomplish great things.

"Destiny is no matter of chance. It is a matter of choice. It is not a thing to be waited for, it is a thing to be achieved."
—William Jennings Bryan

~ CHAPTER 2 ~

The Power and Importance of Pure Choice

Pure Choice: *A concrete decision for which you are completely willing to accept accountability and consequences, whether good or bad; To decide with full acknowledgement of possibilities, uninhibited by external or internal noise; Choosing with what you want in mind (not what others want for you) and as a result being fanatically committed; To target with obsession.*

The Power

"Life happens" a lot less than many of us believe. You know what happens more than life? Our choices. Making a decision begins with recognizing that you have a choice. Say it out loud: "I *always* have a choice!" Many people do not acknowledge this possibility, and in that moment their failure marks the surrendering of their power. Choice *is* power. We choose to read, play, be faithful in relationships, and everything in between. From the seemingly meaningless and often thoughtless decision to put one foot in front of the next as you cross the floor to life-changing decisions such as marriage, our minds are constantly choosing.

Why is choice so powerful? One word: *Freedom*! Even when a choice is wrong, it is freeing. Nothing is more empowering than to know and feel that your fate is in your own hands. Conversely, nothing is worse than feeling, even for a short moment, that someone or something else had a greater influence on your thoughts than your own self. Nothing is more intimate than one's own conscience. For this reason, people despise others who do not give them an opportunity of choice but instead mandate or manipulate their compliance.

Manipulation is especially frowned upon. It bypasses boundaries and infiltrates a person's inner thoughts without that person's knowledge. Manipulation is the ultimate violation. If a person is not destroyed by it, manipulation instills feelings of hatred and revenge—treason at the very least. Outer influences often act as shackles on thoughts, which, by nature, like to move freely. Any deceitful infringement on this freedom engenders bad blood.

Understandably, the thought of controlling your own fate may be frightening in the amount of power it represents, especially considering the possibility of unfavorable results. Even so, making a bad decision *on your own* is far better. Good and bad choices are inevitable. Let the good be yours as well as the bad.

"The wounds and every other evil that men inflict upon themselves spontaneously, and their own choice, are in the long run less painful than those inflicted by others."

–Niccolo Machiavelli

The Importance

We can fail to change something about ourselves over and over again, yet a sudden event can cause us to change forever in a single instant. Even if the change is positive, don't wait for life to happen before you change for the better.

On the Highway

A highway full of cars has a flow of traffic, but each individual has a destination in mind. If you have been driving for any length of time, at some point you have probably experienced driving home and somewhere along the way slipping into "daydream mode." You may have missed a turn, ended up at the wrong place, or perhaps even made it home without vivid recollection of the previous few minutes and how you arrived there.

This experience is incredibly scary. I have been through it and came out thinking, *How could I have* completely *opted out of reality like that? Who knows what could have happened?* Surprisingly, many people live their entire lives this way.

Pure Choice provides a goal. Goals provide direction and clarity. Without true direction we do not adequately question where we are going. If you fail to question your direction, you have no say in your destination. Therefore, when you have not made a choice, you essentially blank out at the wheel and drift along with the flow of traffic in life.

The world is a culmination of forces (people, animals, nature itself), all constantly working to reach individual goals (acting for their own benefit). Most forces do not initially look to work against others but simply find the easiest route to their goal, just as water finds the path of least resistance. This is why a choice must be concrete. Ambiguity is *weak*. If you do not have your own direction in mind, you cannot adequately withstand opposing forces. When you blank out at the wheel and move without purpose, you end up working for someone else's cause. In other words, if you move without purpose, other forces use you for their own.

The world is *never* still. Life pushes you along if you refuse to push yourself, which is why blanking out at the wheel is so dangerous. A detachment from reality usually goes unrecognized until an event snaps you back into awareness. Without any recall of the details between the present and your last awareness, you will have perceivably reached your current state fast, wondering how you got there. The stimulus could be positive, negative, or somewhere in between, but this is a gamble. A person in another car could honk a horn, simply causing you to pay attention, *or* you can haphazardly crash, regaining your attention but also dealing with the additional consequences of your neglect.

Many people go through life wasting time on things that do not collectively move them in any single direction. Consequently, they look up every so often and wonder what they have done with their time. They may not have been lazy. They could, in fact, have been incredibly busy. Still, for all of the energy expended, little or nothing remains to show for it. Do not take that chance. Do not miss your exit. Instead of letting life mold you, mold your life. Otherwise you are in danger of being *busy* but going nowhere. Choose a direction. Set a goal. As you navigate through life and its many distractions, a Pure Choice can be your guiding light. Make choices and move life out of the way.

"If you don't make plans for yourself, you'll probably always fit into someone else's plans"

–Jim Rohn

~ CHAPTER 3 ~

Choose Your Environment

1 + 1 = 5???

I had finally settled down after arriving at my mother's house. I was the only person there, so I turned the television on to the only channel worth watching in the middle of the night: PBS (I was never able to convince my mom to get cable). Tavis Smiley and Will Smith appeared on the screen, sitting in two chairs facing each other and in the midst of an interesting discussion.

It was 2007, and Will Smith's movie *I Am Legend* was soon to come out. Throughout this interview, Smith shared several interesting ideas, but I found one particularly compelling. *"I want to represent possibilities. I want to represent magic . . . that you're in a universe and . . . 2 + 2 only equals 4 if you accept that 2 + 2 equals 4. . . . 2 + 2 is gonna be what I want it to be!"*

Of all the concepts he discussed, I found this one difficult to receive. Although I sensed that I agreed with it, I was unable to translate and apply it to real-life scenarios. Yes, he clearly was alluding to the power of *will* (no pun intended), but using numbers, something so conceptually absolute, seemed to be a poor tool for this analogy. Some time went by with that moment at the back of my head until it suddenly clicked: *It's not the numbers but more the structure and implied rules of an equation that's important!* I thought. This epiphany then made a real-world example far easier to come across.

The Capones

Al Capone wreaked havoc on the Prohibition-era 1920s. Capone grew up in a rough neighborhood in Brooklyn, New York. Already involved in gang life, he left school at the age of fourteen. By the time Capone was thirty he became the target of a rival gang, and Frankie Yale, his "employer," decided it was best for Capone to move to Chicago in order to protect him and his family. While there, he became the protégé of John Torrio, Yale's old mentor and the head of a bootlegging operation. After Torrio passed, Al Capone took over the operation, and the rest is history. He expanded the business, going on to control nightclubs, distilleries, breweries, brothels, gambling joints and several other illegitimate operations—to the tune of a $100 million annual income. Also the figure behind several ruthless murders, Al Capone is easily one of America's most legendary gangsters of all time.

James Capone, Al Capone's oldest brother, not only left school but home altogether at the age of sixteen, moving to Nebraska supposedly to join a circus. Later, he served in the First World War as a lieutenant and then returned to Nebraska, changing his name to Richard James Hart. Hart eventually became a champion of Prohibition, widely known for his successful raids on bootlegging operations—the very business in which his brother thrived—earning the name "Two-Gun Hart." At one point he even became a special agent for the Bureau of Indian Affairs and was responsible for protecting President Calvin Coolidge, again a far cry from his brother's line of work. James Capone was one of the most successful crime-fighters of his time.

What exactly do the Capone brothers have to do with what Will Smith said? When broken down it becomes rather clear. Take two individuals who grew up in the same bad neighborhood around the same time. They went to the same schools and maybe were even raised in the same household. When they grew older, one essentially became a policeman, the other followed a life of crime and ended up dying after serving time in a federal penitentiary.

With that visual, let's simplify $2 + 2 = 4$, to $1 + 1 = 2$. Both individuals had the same "1 + 1" (environmental fundamentals), but their outcomes were different. One's result was "2," the *expected* outcome for an individual growing up in their circumstances. The other's result was a "5"—an extraneous, unexpected outcome. What made the difference? *Choice!* I personally know an individual whose family (siblings, parents, aunts, uncles, cousins) were all criminals, drug addicts, or alcoholics, but this person somehow turned out differently. Some people have every excuse in the world to be the same, but they *choose* to be different.

The Products We Are
In America there is an inherent romanticism in relation to the underdog story—someone who beats the odds and overcomes seemingly insurmountable circumstances. Thanks to capitalism, there are countless examples of individuals whose stories embody this concept. Out of this sort of event comes the very popular phrase, "I am not a product of my environment." That statement is intended to symbolize that beginnings do not determine a final destination in life—a great dogma.

Despite the positive intentions behind "I am not a product of my environment," the statement presents two problems if taken too literally, as some people do. First, it is a lie. We are all affected by our environments. Perhaps we react differently to each circumstance, but we are affected nonetheless. We are the end result of each of our experiences, which are dictated by our environment and the choices we make as we move throughout it. Each action and reaction is what makes people's lives, and each human in general, unique.

This notion is the root of the concept that each person is the average of the five people with whom they spend the most time. Numerically, this statement may not be completely accurate, but the underlying concept is undoubtedly true. No one can fight off all of a person's influence no matter how hard they try. The best solution is to figure out a way to minimize or eliminate any time spent with a negative influence. Furthermore, the people around you are part of your environment, verifying that your surroundings have a profound effect on your outcome. Fortunately, you do not necessarily have to leave the state like James Capone did. Even altering the people you spend time with, the places where you hang out, and your extracurricular activities can make a great difference.

Secondly, "I am not a product of my environment" promotes a subconscious ignorance. Your environment is an inescapable influence, and acknowledging its influence allows you to garner more control over the process. If you admit to yourself that you are a product, then you will pay more attention to the ingredients of your recipe. You will begin to put yourself in line with where you want to go, as opposed to wondering why you are not getting there.

If you do not pay attention to your environment you can only *hope* to end up in a good place. However, when you deliberately influence your environment you *expect* to be exactly where you end up, because you consciously chose to be there.

James Capone controlled his environment. If he remained in the same environment as his brother, he may have been drawn into a criminal lifestyle or at least not realized his full potential as a crime fighter. Instead, he chose to remove himself from the situation into which he was born. This highlights a point of great significance. One's beginning does not determine one's end; more importantly, the choices made in the middle do.

CHAPTER 4

You Always Have a Choice

In 2003 experienced hiker Aron Ralston found himself in an extreme predicament. While descending a canyon in Wayne County, Utah, a boulder became dislodged, pinning him to the canyon wall by his now-crushed right hand. After five days of sparingly consuming water and two burritos, he made a tough decision. Failing to inform anyone of where he would be before he took off on his adventure and out of food, he could no longer rely on being found.

Death was near, but Ralston refused to accept a tragic fate. He used the dull knife of a multitool to cut off half of his forearm, freeing himself from the anchored boulder. He then climbed out of the canyon and began to hike back to his vehicle, losing a great deal of blood as he walked. Fortunately he came across a family on vacation that provided him with food and water as they alerted the authorities. In the time since then, he has written a book, a movie based on his story has been released, and Ralston has had many more outdoor adventures.

In 2007 a farmer was harvesting corn when some stalks got stuck in his corn picker. While the machine was still running, he reached in to remove the stalks from the machine. Suddenly, the picker grabbed hold of his hand and would not let go. No one else was in sight. He yelled for help to no avail. When he attempted to free himself, the machine only pulled him in farther.

Using an iron bar within reach, he jammed the machine but soon came another dilemma. The friction of the iron bar lodged into the machine's gears began to create sparks, setting the ground around him on fire. "My skin was melting. . . . It was dripping off my arm like melting plastic." He used a pocketknife and body weight to tear off his arm and escape. "I told myself I'm not going to die here. . . . I kept fighting, I kept praying," he later confessed in a post-incident interview.

Make no mistake, outside of pure insanity, neither of these situations could be overcome in the ways they were without Pure Choice. Even if someone completely believed that such an action would save one's life, cutting off a limb so battles our nature that it would not be possible to do so without complete commitment. A partially committed individual may be able to cut into an arm somewhat, but would probably be unsuccessful in severing it entirely.

This type of action has to be bold. This type of action must be forceful. Otherwise, the level of applied pressure needed to complete the goal is never achieved. It is like tearing a thick stack of papers. You cannot nonchalantly pull the papers in half. You must concentrate on a certain point and be swift in your motion in order to tear them significantly.

In cases like these, indecisive action causes more pain than definitive, devoted decision. The same often reigns true in the less extreme circumstances of our everyday lives. Indecision is not only less effective in completing a task, but the additional pain or failure can be disheartening, making it even harder to press onward. The aforementioned stories clearly call for a choice uninhibited by mental obstacles, but the power of Pure Choice is not reserved for dire circumstances.

Commit fanatically to a cause and you will figure out how to reach your destination in ways you would have never thought possible. As extreme as the prior examples may seem, they paint a clear picture that, as individuals, we *always* have a choice. Unfortunately, many people relinquish their choices by choosing to believe that none are available.

"Decision is a sharp knife that cuts clean and straight; indecision, a dull one that hacks and tears and leaves ragged edges behind it."— Gordon Graham

Summary of Core 1: Pure Choice

1. **The power of choice.**
   a. Choice is *freedom*! Although it may be scary at first, when you take charge of your own life you do not feel imprisoned by your circumstances. Moreover, your fate is not left to someone else's discretion.

2. **Everything begins with a choice.**
   a. Your life is a culmination of choices. If you want to change your life, then change your choices.
   b. You *always* have a choice.

3. **Pure Choice is the only way to combat life.**
   a. A Pure Choice is a concrete goal or standard that one has fully committed to reaching, regardless of the obstacles faced.
   b. So many forces in this world are trying to achieve their own goals. If you have no will of your own, these forces will impress their will upon you. Set a new standard. Choose the life you want to live and map your way in the world.

4. **Your environment matters.**
   a. Your influences are a product of your environment, and so are your options. Choose surroundings that help you achieve your goals.

Core 2

Mindset

~ CHAPTER 5 ~

The Most Powerful Weapon

Fear is often cited as the most powerful weapon there is. Why? Because it limits the mind. Still, individuals who are able to tap deep enough into their mental strength can easily overcome fear. If for no more than this reason alone, *the mind*—not fear—is the most powerful weapon.

Think about it this way; the mind is the command center for everything. Minds have created nuclear weapons and fighter jets, composed music and assembled computers, formed armies and built civilizations. Many things—from frightening to fun—originated in thought. The beauty in this perspective is that everyone has a mind.

Clearly, an individual who learns how to use this weapon is well served. If you want success in whatever you choose, getting there is simple as well as hard—simple in the sense that all you have to do is train your mind, hard in the sense that the training and actions on the journey to achievement are not easy.

A quarterback must be able to complete throws under a variety of conditions to master his position. Musicians must learn many scales and chords to master their instrument. Similarly, you can use different mindsets to master the weapon that is your mind.

Once you have made a choice, assisting and debilitating states of thought will respectively help or hurt your chances of success. Being aware of these different states will make your journey far easier. In fact, in most instances success is not possible without proper attention to these mindsets. Although Pure Choice is powerful, the human mind has the ability to hinder Pure Choice to the point that a person's actions are completely contradictory to one's goal.

~ CHAPTER 6 ~

You Only Have One Filter

"If you always put limits on everything you do, physical or anything else, it will spread into your work and into your life."
—Bruce Lee

The subconscious is like the operating system on a computer. It is always running in the background. Just as several specialized organs come together and harmoniously serve one human body, a person's specific thoughts culminate into one filter through which everything manifests. Although humans are gifted with the ability to perceive vicariously, personal perception ultimately defers to this one filter, no matter what.

When you are not deliberately overriding your subconscious with intentions, your filter holds an overwhelming influence on your perception. This is the idea being referred to by labels such as *optimist* and *pessimist*. These words generalize a person's perceptual habits. Both approaches have a certain outlook for seeing the world, each equally real to the respective individual.

Fortunately humans are also gifted with self-revision: the ability to change oneself. To do so effectively you must edit your thoughts. Bruce Lee's quote at the beginning of the chapter alludes to why rewriting poor thinking habits is important. Thoughts are viruses. If you water a bad seed, you face the dangerous reality that the seed will grow into your perception and, consequently, negatively affect your life. Martin Luther King Jr. understood this as well when he famously proclaimed, "Injustice anywhere is a threat to justice everywhere." Ideas seek to grow and be transferred, so you must pay close attention to the thoughts you entertain in order to prevent cancerous thoughts from spreading.

Changing your life starts here. The exercise of changing perception is important because of the mental conditioning it affords and the subsequent snowball effect it will have. Every action in life originates in the mind. You *make* happen what you, somewhere within, feel needs to happen. This applies from the far-reaching metaphysical sense of the law of attraction down to the easy-to-grasp connection between thinking *I'm hungry* and then eating pizza.

Options only exist to the extent of perception. Consequently, your view of the world around you determines what you do in that world. You only have one filter, so take heed of how you condition it. That filter determines the thought process you apply to *every* area in life.

Change Now!
If you want change in your life, then first *you* must change. People often continue poor behaviors but expect something to happen in order to fix their problems. Have you ever heard anything similar to these phrases?

- "I'll learn how to manage money when I get rich."

- "I'll start working hard when I get a job I like."

- "I'll give 100 percent when the game starts."

Change doesn't work this way; change begins within. If you want something, increase your capacity to handle it. Your filter controls how you think and ultimately how you act. Put another way, the standards of your actions are held to the standards of your mind. The amount of money a person has only determines the amount of flexibility that person has to exercise her money management skills. If you are bad with money, getting rich only gives you more money to manage poorly.

The process of conditioning your mind is like practicing for anything else. You cannot rationally expect to play to a standard for which you did not adequately practice. Look at the individuals considered to be the greatest of all time in their respective fields and you will find them to have practiced the hardest. You must give a 100 percent effort in practice in order to give a 100 percent effort in the game. As Aristotle once said, "We are what we repeatedly do. Excellence therefore is not an act but a habit."

Just as dropping a habit cold turkey is difficult, hastily gaining a new habit is equally difficult. You must be persistent. Humans are creatures of habit, and what we do is only the end result of what we think. As stated before, thoughts are viruses that infect people's lives; whether that is a good thing is up to you. Your mind allows user input, so program it as you please.

"Once you change your philosophy, you change your thought pattern. Once you change your thought pattern you change your attitude. Once you change your attitude it changes your behavior pattern...As long as you've got a sit-down philosophy, you'll have a sit-down thought pattern, and as long as you think that old sit-down thought, you'll be in some kind of sit down action. It'll have you sitting-in everywhere" –Malcolm X

Part A

The 4 Mindsets of Failure

~ CHAPTER 7 ~

Mindset #1: Fear

You have probably heard how fear can detrimentally affect various aspects of a person's life. The same reigns true when it comes to Pure Choice. Fear is the most hindering state of being that exists. It can cause you to select an option completely contrary to your desires, damaging logic as well as dreams. If left unchecked, fear will run rampant in every decision you make.

The Effect of Fear on Choice

In 1820 the whaleship *Essex* faced a whale attack that left it to sink. After salvaging what supplies they could, twenty surviving sailors set out in three small boats. The closest known land was the Marquesas Islands. Captain George Pollard intended to head for them, but the Marquesas were rumored to be inhabited by cannibals and the crew voted otherwise. Instead, they decided to head to South America, a journey they knew would likely stretch their already contaminated food supply. In the end, only eight men survived. Ironically, when they ran out of food on their journey, they resorted to cannibalism.

A popular question this story poses is as follows: If the men had simply set sail to the Marquesas, would all twenty men have survived? Many have speculated the answer to be yes. It was only rumored that cannibals occupied the Marquesas, but many of the sailors were experienced enough to *know* they did not have enough food to last the journey to South America. So why did they choose to take the longer voyage to South America? *Fear.*

In observance of this story, fiction writer Karen Thompson Walker suggests that fear causes people to ignore the actual likelihood of all outcomes and focus on the scenarios they consider to be more tragic or scary. People tend to be more affected by outcomes they can imagine better. The more graphic the images the mind conceives, the more real they are to a person. More importantly, the more real they *feel*. For this reason, the sailors responded greater to the fear of violence (i.e., cannibalism) than starvation, a happening that is difficult to imagine in detail.

Fear in Time
All choices can be categorized in two basic groups: past-present (*What should I do now?*) and past-future (*What should I do later?*). *Past-present* refers to the extremely urgent, short-term future. These decisions at their purest are a quick and instinctive analysis of the past to provoke immediate action. There is no time to reach deep into the past in order to analyze a situation thoroughly. A common example of past-present decision making is fight or flight, which is often considered a good thing since it is necessary for survival.

Past-future decisions concern analyzing the past and making decisions about circumstances that are less urgent. The amount of time between the present and the point in time when a decision will be necessary is either long or indefinite. Therefore, time for more sensible analysis is available, unless fear enters the mind.

Fear feeds on imagination, motivating decisions through fabricated possibilities as opposed to rational thought. More time affords the imagination the chance to paint pictures in greater detail. As noted earlier, vivid images tend to take priority. For this reason, fear threatens to dilute logic over time. The following figure depicts the fundamental effects of fear and urgency on our choices.

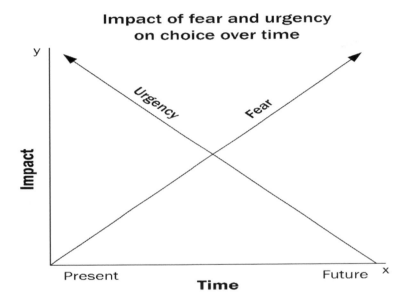

Impact of fear and urgency on choice over time

A circumstance can be placed at any given point in time on this scale. As time passes, the circumstance moves left along the x-axis, slowly transitioning from a past-future into a past-present decision as its urgency rises. If you are too inflicted by fear at that point, the likelihood of a good decision decreases by several times. Even worse, if a choice is not necessary and totally up to you (e.g., self-improvement), you may be stuck in a constant state of indecision, afraid of what your choice might mean. Fear can be paralyzing.

'Most people don't have the guts to make the tough decisions, because they want to make the right decision, so they

make NO decision…and that's a decision." –Tony Robbins

Bringing fear back into the perspective of circumstances may allow you to relate more: Why take two years to decide whether to act on an idea that would have taken only six months to fail? Why take two years to make a decision that would have been successful after one year and acting on it is probably now out of the question? Even worse, why risk someone else following through and reaping the fruits of *your* vision? You can always find a reason to delay. Either choose to pursue an opportunity or move on to the next one. If anything, do not get analysis paralysis.

Far too often, people allow the most frightening images to eclipse the possibility of a positive outcome. As a result, they focus more on preventing the fruition of their fears than pursuing the materialization of their dreams. When successful people reflect, they usually express bewilderment at how ignorant they were to the obstacles they would have to face on their respective journeys.

Moreover, they admit that if they knew of the challenges beforehand, they probably would never have pursued their goal. At some point, due diligence subjects you to diminishing returns if no action is taken. Do not let fear stop you. Learn enough to decide and continue to learn along the way in order to make proper adjustments if necessary. Otherwise, fear will leave you stationary or even backpedaling. Fear is stagnant; failure is progress. As Franklin D. Roosevelt in his first inaugural address so famously paraphrased Sir Francis Bacon, "The only thing we have to fear is fear itself."

~ CHAPTER 8 ~

Mindset #2: Insecurity (Lack of Confidence)

Insecurity is almost completely self-explanatory. It essentially means someone is lacking in confidence. Insecurity can apply to someone's entire mental thought process or something more specific, such as approaching the opposite sex or public speaking. Sometimes individuals fail to pursue a choice solely because of a lack of confidence. Insecurities are incredible in how unique they are. People can be insecure about anything.

People can even be insecure about things that seemingly do not apply to them. Many people possess an enviable trait, yet they feel that particular attribute is, for whatever reason, inadequate. The problem is that insecurities are often cloaked as fact.

I can't, I'm not, They won't, It doesn't. . . . No matter how many compliments a person may receive, an obstacle in the brain simply says, *Not true.* The problem is that a lack of confidence weakens performance. Even if something is done well without confidence, having confidence guarantees better performance.

Insecurity is a breeding ground for fear. Moreover, just as fear is often a gross exaggeration, insecurity is often an exaggeration or an outright lie. Even if insecurity is somewhat infrequent, the danger is in the possibility that lack of confidence will come into play when it matters the most.

Do not miss out on a great opportunity because you were not confident enough to act. Perhaps you have a work-related suggestion that you do not feel enough confidence to relay because the idea seems far-fetched. Maybe you're facing an opportunity that you do not pursue because you feel you do not have what it takes. Any of these could be the one idea or action that changes your career, family, or love life for the better. Of course, all fears and insecurities may not be possible to eliminate. The key is to use them positively. If you cannot get rid of them, find enough comfort in your fear or insecurity to attack your goal with a level head and propel you forward.

"You can't do your best when you're doubting yourself"

–Michael Jackson

~ CHAPTER 9 ~

Mindset #3: Naivety of Personal Limitation

Naivety can be the most difficult state of being to address because it is hard for a person to detect one's own ignorance. Fear takes over so intensely and so completely that it becomes tangible. Insecurity comes to life through anxiety, awkwardness, and several other emotions that are equally palpable. However, if you are ignorant of something, how do you know? It is not always as simple as needing to look up the definition of an unfamiliar word. Perhaps you have a bad practice that needs to be stopped or a best practice that you don't use enough. Something internal or external could be affecting you without you even realizing it.

Whatever it is, you are not aware, and as a result the issue is being neglected. If you fail to pay attention to your environment's reaction to your actions and vice versa, you are not only doomed to repeat your wrongs but sure to be unaware of what you do right. Sometimes people fall into a routine so comfortable that they no longer see the need for improvement until life *requires* better. Other times, people fail to recognize need for change because they "have it all figured out." Two common brands of naivety that can keep you from reaching your goals are "know-it-all" and "do-it-all."

You Know It All...Until You Don't

When reminiscing about their younger selves, people tend to more readily acknowledge their lack of awareness. As a matter of fact, they *expect* to do so. People often find humor in their youthful naivety. As adults, however, the tendency is to feel completely aware of and on guard against the ideas, dangers, joys, and experiences of everyday life, which is why this trend of naivety frequently continues into adulthood. That presumptuous assuredness is what leads people to, once again, be surprised years later at how oblivious they were.

Forty-year-olds consider themselves more in tune with themselves than their thirty-year-old counterparts. Thirty-year-olds laugh at the immature, twenty-year-old versions of themselves. Twenty-year-olds are amazed at how things that are grossly unimportant in hindsight meant so much at the age of fifteen, and so on. To most people, a lack of awareness is forever a phenomenon of the past. Consequently, most individuals let circumstances initiate self-reflection as opposed to regulating this process themselves (which, you may remember from earlier in the book, is not a good thing). Do not wait until an impetus incites deeper thought, but instead make self-reflection an ongoing, habitual life practice.

Contrary to popular belief, you never completely know yourself. There is no final test for which you receive a certificate proclaiming, "Congratulations! You know exactly who you are!" The magical occurrence of knowing *exactly* who you are lasts only as long as it takes for the next second to arrive. People change constantly. Moreover, the pace of change never remains the same.

There is not only the inevitable natural progression of life but also individual events that hold varying weights in how they affect us. The closest thing you will ever have to this elusive aha moment is when you have a strong sense of your core values and an accepted comfort with *not* knowing yourself in the sense that we normally consider to be complete. At first this notion might sound depressing, but if you are not growing, you are dying.

Again, because of this perpetual change, knowing who you are at this second is not to know who you are a year or even days from now. Frequent self-reflection is a way to catch up with your ever-changing self and ensure that you do not fall too far behind. Never fall into the trap of feeling that you have arrived. You always have more to learn about yourself and your craft. If you fail to recognize that you do not know it all, you are likely to be unaware of your shortcomings.

"I can't go back to yesterday, because I was a different person then"–Lewis Carroll

Another huge naivety, partly a result of the aforementioned issue, is not knowing what type of help you need. Even worse is thinking you need no help at all. Time is limited. To use it efficiently, bring in other people. Additionally, being naive of your naivety (being a know-it-all) and ignoring other people's words will restrict your growth. Our minds feed off of other people's ideas.

Although so much of personal success is due to internal development, external factors, especially people, play a significant role. When employed skillfully, people can make your journey a lot smoother. Obstacles are inevitable, and creativity is the most effective way to get around them. Being a know-it-all closes the mind and hinders creativity.

For The Do-it-all: Why Outer Influence Is Necessary

You will never be the best you without other people. There is simply not enough time for one person to acquire the number of perspectives that empower creativity. Other people allow you to save time by offering theirs.

Perspective and Knowledge

Think about how long it would have taken you to learn everything you know without school, your parents, friends, or anybody else. To be extreme, imagine you were left alone on an island at birth. If you happened to survive, consider how long it would take to learn a single subject such as math. You would not only have to learn math, you would have to *invent* it.

Thankfully, the human race has already learned so many things over the years. It only makes sense to leverage others' knowledge, which is the function of school, books, conversation, and human interaction in general. The exchange of information is the cornerstone of human civilization's advancement. For this reason, a huge gap exists between *what you can do* and *what you can do alone.*

You've likely heard the phrase, "Have a fresh pair of eyes look at it." The idiom acknowledges the typical occurrence of someone who works on a task endlessly only to have another individual enter and instantly solve the problem. Surely you have been involved in at least one side of this situation, a classic example of perspective at work.

A friend of mine once had a puzzle he wanted me to try and solve. Unfortunately, I could not figure it out, so he showed me; of course, the answer was extremely simple. This is the power of additional perception. My friend essentially transferred his point of view and saved me a significant amount of time. He did, however, spend a significant amount of time figuring it out himself, so in a sense, he gave me time. I got the answer as if I invested the hours to figure it out. Moreover, he gave me a point of view of a particular circumstance that I will never lose. Now, whenever I see the puzzle, I solve it effortlessly. It literally takes less than two seconds. The time my friend "gave" or "saved" me shows why information exchange is so powerful. Time saved from working on one problem can be used on the next.

Perspective and Creativity

People often go to extremes in search of creativity. They either look too far outside of themselves, as if some magical epiphany will take place, or they look too deeply within, to the point that the search becomes stressful, counterproductive, and head-splitting. Just as with knowledge, other people can help in the creative process.

In an interview, Steve Jobs said something about creativity that highlighted why so many people struggle with it: "Creativity is just connecting things." This sounded great when I first read it (probably because Steve Jobs said it), but the impact did not take place until I constantly evaluated myself with Jobs's statement in mind. It finally clicked when I realized, "I'm *naturally* creative!" We all are.

I would always think of new ideas by putting my own twist on what people said and thought nothing of it until other people pointed it out. Because of my personal filter, my perception was and still is unique in many ways. My problem was that whenever I consciously decided, *I want to be creative*, I would go in a mental hole, block out the world, and search for the most Einsteinian moment of genius the world has seen since Einstein himself: the wrong approach.

As stated earlier in the book, everyone has their own filter. *No one* can help this. *Everyone* should use it to their advantage. People do not usually identify most of their own thoughts as unique. Some thoughts are so obvious to them, they wrongly assume that everybody must think that way.

With that in mind, a key to being creative is paying attention to your own thoughts in reaction to what you see or hear. Creative thoughts come most easily through conversation and observation. All you have to do is listen to others and then listen to yourself. As with knowledge, people need people to maximize creative potential. Creativity is not coming up with new ideas. Creativity is taking old ideas and putting them together in new ways. The mother of your greatest idea is someone else's idea.

~ CHAPTER 10 ~

Mindset #4: Short-sightedness

The problem with shortsightedness is that it wrongly diminishes the value of sacrifice. There are so many phrases such as "YOLO" (You Only Live Once), "Live Fast, Die Young," "Live Every Day Like It's Your Last"—the list goes on and on. These phrases *should* be a reminder to show gratitude each day and not to live life in fear. More often, they are interpreted as an excuse for a lack of a commitment to a long-term vision, especially in the young adult demographic. Chris Rock summed this issue up best:

> "You know, some people say life is short and
> that you could get hit by a bus at any moment
> and that you have to live each day like it's
> your last. Bullshit! Life is looong. You're
> probably not gonna get hit by a bus and
> you're gonna have to live with the choices
> you made for the next fifty years."

The average U.S. life expectancy as reported by the Centers for Disease Control and Prevention (CDC) is almost seventy-nine years old. For third-world countries, the life expectancy is closer to fifty-six years old.

The chances of living to be seventy-nine is one of the seemingly few positive statistics. Why would someone want to be the "exception" to it? If there is any time to be a statistic, living a long life– seventy-nine years –is it. Save being an exception for times when the cards are stacked *against* you. Strive to be an exception to a statistic that insists success is not likely.

Perhaps realizing there are many years to come will make it easier to envision a destination five, ten, or fifteen years down the road. At that point, undergoing the preparation and sacrifice necessary to achieve your vision of success will begin to make a lot more sense. Tomorrow's successes require sacrifices today. If you do not choose with the future in mind, you will never experience the today you desire.

The Value of Time

If you won $50,000 and had the choice of receiving it today or three years from now, which would you choose?

If you are like most people, you would choose "today" without a doubt. Some people may have said this because they would not trust that the offer would still be good after three years. Some may *really need* $50,000 at the moment. There are probably countless valid reasons for taking the money sooner than later, but one is especially noteworthy: *the time value of money.*

The idea of the time value of money is that a set amount of money is always worth more today than it is tomorrow. "I can make better use of the money than you can, so it doesn't make sense for me to let you hold on to it." This concept drives financial philosophy. A popular rationale for this concept is simple: *take advantage of compound interest.*

Compound interest is an amazing way to multiply money. If money is invested wisely, interest can be earned on the original amount, and if continually reinvested at the end of a period (e.g., a year), more interest can be gained on the sum of the original amount plus earned interest. Put another way, interest is continually earned on top of interest.

For example, consider if you took that $50,000 today and invested it at a 10 percent interest rate for three years. The table below displays the result of this investment. (The interest rate used is for illustration purposes only and does not necessarily indicate market interest rates at the time of publication.)

Year	Principal	Interest Earned	Total
1	$ 50,000	$ 5,000	$ 55,000
2	$ 55,000	$ 5,500	$ 60,500
3	$ 60,500	$ 6,050	$ 66,550

Notice the total at the end of the third year is $66,550—a total of $16,550 more than you would have had if you waited until the third year to receive your money. Even worse, the possibility of inflation risks the $50,000 being worth *less* than it was in Year 1. So as you can see, getting your money up front is the right way to go.

Why is this important? Because choices are the same way. As a matter of fact, in the prior example, taking the money immediately and investing it as opposed to waiting *is* a choice. Every choice is an investment of your time. Just as money does, the effects of your choices compound in your life. Consider this as the *time value of choice*. A positive choice made today is worth more than a positive choice tomorrow. The individual who sacrifices trivial things to invest in a goal now will have received a greater value than the person who did not choose to do so until later. This point applies not only to achievement but prevention. For instance, quitting smoking after two years is better than quitting after twenty. Why? Because the negative effects of the carcinogens will have compounded for a greater amount of time. Therefore, the potential damage is exponentially worse. With that said, choosing not to smoke at all would obviously trump both situations.

Always make sure you are able to see past the short term and over the horizon. Long-term vision is a guidance mechanism to ensure that time is invested wisely. Here is where your Pure Choice comes into play. It only makes sense that your choices coincide with your Pure Choice. Each day, your actions should get you closer to your ultimate goal. If you are not willing to sacrifice in the short term to achieve your goal, then it will forever remain a dream.

Summary of The 4 Mindsets of Failure

1. **Your mind is your most powerful weapon.**
   a. Every great feat humans have accomplished is a product of the mind.
   b. When used skillfully, nothing can keep a mind from success.

2. **You only have one filter.** Each individual filters all thoughts through a unique perceptual filter.
   a. You see everything with the same set of eyes, which controls how you approach life as a whole.
   b. If you want a change in life, change your thoughts and perception.

3. **Fear** dilutes logical decision making.
   a. Fear not only keeps people from taking action but can also cause people to make poorer decisions and take *bad* action.

4. **Insecurity (a lack of confidence)** has a negative effect on performance.
   a. We often present our insecurities as facts to make them seem real. People may say, "I can't," simply because they are afraid to try.
   b. You cannot perform at your best without confidence.

5. **Naivety** stunts growth. We never know as much as we think.
   a. There is danger in thinking we have everything figured out, no matter what age we are. Self-reflection helps you avoid this mentality and allows you to find areas where you can grow.

b. Danger lurks in thinking that you can do everything alone. You need other people to get to your maximum potential. It would take far more time for one mind to accomplish what many can together.

6. **Shortsightedness** is another ingredient of bad decision making.

   a. If you do not choose with the future in mind, you will never experience the today you desire.

   b. There is a *time value of choice*. Good choices are better made now than later. The longer you wait to make a good choice or sacrifice, the less value you will be able to experience from it.

Part B

The 4 Mindsets of Achievement

~ CHAPTER 11 ~

Mindset #1: Self-accountability

My life is my fault. It may sound weird but that statement offers a vital mindset for achievement. When you face obstacles, you do not fail because they are there, but because you have not acquired the abilities necessary to overcome them. An individual has sole responsibility to bring her goals into fruition. If you do not accept this responsibility, then you are at risk of becoming a victim in life.

Victims do not achieve success because, so they say, some external forces actively prevented them from doing so. The truth is that they allow forces to hold them back. If you do not look internally first, you will never develop the attributes needed to obtain what you desire. People may change jobs, cities, and even countries and still find themselves dissatisfied. When life is your fault, within is the first place you look for problems as well as solutions. As some people say, "You are your biggest obstacle. No one can stop you but you." In order to consistently fend off external forces, you must nurture your inner forces. Keep this in mind and never be the reason you do not achieve success.

Taking full accountability for your successes and failures allows you to become better. It forces you to step up to the plate because no one else is to blame. A person may have truly done you wrong, but blaming someone else is never any more than an excuse for you not to become better. "I'm already good enough, but that person has something against me"—this statement suggests that the only thing that needs to change is the individual or obstacle in your way. The problem is that an obstacle may exist for years—maybe even a lifetime.

As a child, Richard Branson found school completely frustrating. His attempts to understand traditional schoolwork were hopeless. "I decided that at a very young age I needed to get out of this environment and, you know, . . . carve my own way in life." At the time, he did not know that he had dyslexia, a developmental reading disorder. Many years later at the age of fifty, prompted by an employee's inquiry, the billionaire admitted to not knowing the difference between "net" and "gross," two of the most fundamental business concepts. Luckily, he knew how to hire people who did.

Remarkably, Branson made a decision to overcome his obstacle *before* he could define it. Who knows? Maybe he would have used his learning disability as an excuse if he was treated like he had a disorder. Still, great numbers of people with disabilities and disorders have reached heights beyond what was expected of them. Watch the news, search the Internet. The stories are endless. When you make a choice to carve your own way in life as Branson did, your fate is in your own hands. It then becomes second nature when facing obstacles to compensate in whatever way necessary to succeed.

Michael Jordan was also well aware of the connection between self-accountability, compensation, and overcoming obstacles. After years of being the National Basketball Association's most explosive player and winning three consecutive championships with the Chicago Bulls, Jordan left the game of basketball. However, his retirement was short-lived. He returned to the league a different man two years later. Jordan knew that he could not continue performing at the level he was accustomed to with the same style of play. He was older, and his body would not be able to take regular beatings as it had in prior years.

Jordan worked to evolve his game from a fierce aerial attack to that of a methodical, grounded killer. He worked to improve his jump shot and mastered his famous "fade away," allowing him to score without putting as much stress on his body. At the tail end of his professional career, he won three more championships.

Age was a roadblock, but Jordan was determined to find his way around it. He had already reached the perceived pinnacle of his sport, yet he pushed to raise the bar even higher. Michael Jordan knew his goal (championships) and acquired the abilities necessary to achieve them.

Obstacles in Society

When encountering social obstacles such as gender, race, class, or age, the responsibility is still yours to achieve, no matter what. More than strictly objective or physical obstacles (competition, transportation, money, time, or distance), the enormity of discriminatory obstacles is often amplified in the mind of affected individuals. People have a psychological tendency to magnify the size of these perceived barriers. In this case, the greatest enemy is not the source of discrimination but the individual. While discriminatory obstacles are very real, if you empower them beyond their actual ability, you are hurting yourself. Do not add bricks to a wall you are trying to climb.

Racism, sexism, classism, and other discriminatory obstacles should be looked at as merely "another obstacle," holding no more weight than a lack of resources, competition or any other handicap or hurdle imaginable. Spending energy railing against any external factor is a waste of time and a distraction from your goal. Unless your primary initiative is to abolish that particular external factor (e.g., Martin Luther King Jr. and racism), redirect your focus away from it and toward your goal instead. With that said, King refused to allow even racism itself to stop him from overcoming racism.

Madame C. J. Walker, born poor in 1867, is considered the first self-made female millionaire in American history. As an African American woman, she started a business in 1907, at a time when discrimination could not get much stronger. Presidents Richard Nixon and Abraham Lincoln grew up poor on farms. President Barack Obama had no example of an African American president before him and could have labeled his pursuit of the office as an impossibility.

Sheryl Sandberg is currently the chief operating officer of Facebook, and Indra Nooyi, who was born and raised in India, is the chief executive officer of Pepsico. Both are women in male-dominated industries commonly considered to be immersed in sexist traditions. Ray Charles, the legendary musician, had a disability with serious physical and social ramifications.

When Will Smith was set to star in *Independence Day*, the president of Twentieth-Century Fox at the time wanted to replace Smith with a white actor due to the misconception that summer blockbuster movies could not have a black male lead and make money. At the time this text is being written Smith has starred in twelve blockbusters, each grossing at least $100 million at the box office, including *Independence Day*.

These people, who could have used one or several social

roadblocks as an excuse, achieved anyway. The truth is that when you aim high, obstacles are such a regular occurrence that you become used to sizing them up and knocking them down. Most limitations that exist for us are limitations that we allow to exist. Once you recognize this fact, you will be on the fast track to achieving your goals. You will be able to find your way around obstacles faster because you will not be blinded by the deceit of something being someone else's fault. The first step is already out of the way. You know where to start: *within*.

You, not others, are ultimately in control of what you become. Physical and social obstacles are mere hurdles, not barriers. Molding yourself in order to achieve what you want to achieve is up to you. Fair or unfair, obstacles are tests that only exist to make you better and weed out those who are not willing to put in the required effort to achieve.

Educate yourself and acquire whatever skills in whatever ways possible to get where you need to be. You have the capacity to build and rebuild who you are. You are responsible for preparing your own self for war, so add weapons to your arsenal. Like Michael Jordan, if you run into an obstacle, do not be discouraged. . . . Develop a jump shot.

"Remind yourself. Nobody's built like you, you design yourself..."

–Jay Z

~ CHAPTER 12 ~

Mindset #2: The Law of Focus

"I fear not the man who has practiced 10,000 kicks once, but the man who has practiced one kick 10,000 times." –Bruce Lee

Focus and Achievement

I once sat in on a program where talk show and game show host Steve Harvey was the keynote speaker. In his speech he acknowledged a vital mindset of high achievement. Harvey explained that "Don't put all your eggs in one basket" is common but bad advice and arouses an anti-success mentality, especially if you are seeking huge success. It is true, the higher you are reaching, the worse this advice is. "You can't reach great success at anything without giving 110 percent! Time is limited. If I'm spending time on too many things I'm not going to be able to make any significant ground on any of them!" he exhorted. When his statements were challenged with, "What do you do if you fail?" he quipped, "I just find another basket. . . . I choose something else and I give it 110 percent."

For individuals who perform at high levels, the truth in this philosophy is clear. High performers have a deep focus and show contempt toward the idea of failure being anything more than redirection. Diversification has its merits, but when starting from ground zero, diversification is of little worth. Besides, what do you have to diversify on ground zero? Strategic diversification is a method best left for assuring longevity *after* establishing oneself in one arena.

Some people desperately want to be rich and are consequently always looking for the next big thing to make that happen. The problem with these people is that they usually never stick with anything long enough to reap the benefits.

Imagine a man decides he would like to drill for oil. He figures he does not want to waste too much time in one spot under the sole belief that the more holes he drills, the better chance he has to strike. Because of this, he drills hole after hole about five thousand feet deep. What if all of the oil is six thousand feet deep?

Yes, it would take more time to have drilled an extra thousand feet, but it would be less time than it takes to drill another five-thousand-foot hole, especially considering the time it takes to gather and set up equipment in a new location. Unless he changes, this man will forever be one thousand feet from success.

Many people, unfortunately, use this approach, hoping to get rich quick. Instead of going deep, they go wide, opting for quantity over quality, inconstancy over fidelity and as a result, are distracted by novelty instead of pursuing mastery. After putting energy into an opportunity, its novelty wears off. When obstacles arrive, other opportunities begin to look more promising, but focus is needed more than ever at that point. If you intend to take full advantage of a great opportunity, you will have to turn down a lot of great opportunities. Tune out all distractions and focus on your goal. If you are focusing on many things, you are not focusing.

"I was taught that the strategy to get rich—take concentrated risk, typically with your labor capital/business—is entirely different than the strategy to stay rich, which is to minimize the risks we take, diversify the ones we take as much as possible, keep costs low, tax efficiency high, and don't spend too much."

—Larry Swedroe

A Secret Power of Focus: Bending Time

One summer night I went out with a few friends. After a night a group of college guys would deem a success, we all returned to my friend's house (where we initially met up for the night) and got into our respective cars. I was the first to drive away.

On the way home, I suddenly realized that I had only slept for about eight hours over the previous three days. Of course, I only noticed this after feeling the pain of trying to stay awake. I even considered pulling over, but by that time I was less than five minutes away from my dad's house. *Fight it! At least there aren't any other cars on the road to worry about.* I looked at the time: 2:15 a.m. Euphoria then took over as I envisioned the workless, school-less day ahead of me and all of the sleep I would get. . . .

I opened my eyes and stared at the clock—still 2:15 a.m. Something was strange, though. There was an eerily peaceful nothingness. I was weightless. . . . My focus switched to the windshield and only grass and concrete could be seen through it. . . . *I'm in the air!* As quickly as the thought came, the grill of the car landed, what seemed to be softly, onto a curb. Suddenly the world around me became white amid a violent shattering of glass. A dusty smoke exploded into my face as something flashed red and heat raced through my arms. An instant later, sitting in my seat, I realized I had never seen an airbag before. *Was that an airbag? I guess those things are real*, and screamed in a way so unlike myself and out of my control it sounded inhuman to me. . . . This all happened in what seemed to be a few minutes. Logic dictates that it was only a matter of seconds.

* * * * *

BBC broadcaster and psychology lecturer Claudia Hammond explored the phenomenon of an individual's varying perception of time in her book *Time Warped: Unlocking the Mysteries of Time Perception*. In consideration of the idea that we are most likely to vividly remember experiences that occurred between the ages of fifteen and twenty-five, Hammond argues, "The reason we remember our youth so well is that it is a period where we have more new experiences than in our thirties or forties. It's a time for firsts—first sexual relationships, first jobs, first travel without parents, first experience of living away from home, the first time we get much real choice over the way we spend our days."

First-time instances are unfamiliar to us, causing us to pay more attention to details that we may later overlook as insignificant. To get a better understanding of this concept, consider the 2011 *New Yorker* profile of neuroscientist David Eagleman, written by Burkhard Bilger. Eagleman notes that in life-threatening circumstances the human mind goes into overdrive, recording the present in extreme detail. Eagleman also insists that the length of time a moment seems to last positively correlates with the amount of detail absorbed.

In short, more detail equals more time. Eagleman asserts that this concept "explains why we think that time speeds up when we grow older . . . why childhood summers seem to go on forever, while old age slips by while we're dozing."

In the case of my accident, at twenty-one years old I was almost dead center in Hammond's fifteen-to-twenty-five age range, it was indeed my first car wreck, and it was obviously the sort of life-threatening situation Eagleman described. All of these factors probably caused me to be hyper-attentive, soaking up detail after detail of the incident and perceivably slowing time down as a result (See Appendix C).

Questions Help You Focus

I actually could have described the event of my accident in far greater detail if necessary. Seconds felt like minutes, highlighting the power of something that we can control ourselves: *asking questions*. The idea is not meant to be taken as a simple instruction to question how, who, why, what, or when, but also a reminder to put yourself in positions that inspire your natural curiosity. New experiences automatically make us curious: new smells, sounds, places, people, and subject matter. In her book Claudia Hammond even suggested that people who have changed careers or went through an equivalent lifestyle change (e.g., divorce, city change) later in life showed a resurgence of the longer-lasting, vivid remembrances of their youthful years.

Conscious questioning is the most powerful way to combat detachment from the present in your everyday routine. In the *New Yorker* profile mentioned earlier, Burkhard Bilger wrote, "The more familiar the world becomes, the less information your brain writes down, and the more quickly time seems to pass." Questions keep you grounded in your environment by encouraging observation. They force you to focus as you search for an answer by taking in more detail to beef up your analysis.

When watching a new movie there is always a question of what's going to happen next, and consequently people pay close attention. This attention to detail explains why movies usually feel much longer than they actually are. Movies are experiential submersions. Viewers are deeply focused.

When people speak of "life" pushing them around, they are really referring to two things: how fast time flies and the absence of choice in that time. Both are matters of perception. We've already covered that there is always a choice. Now you understand how details allow you to slow down and take charge of your time. Fight perception with perception. Do not get pushed around at the speed of life. You might not be able to *buy* more time, but if you pay attention, you tend to *have* more of it.

~ CHAPTER 13 ~

Mindset #3: Perseverance

"Dripping water hollows out stone, not through force but through persistence." –Ovid

In so many ways, focus and perseverance go hand in hand. As a matter of fact, perseverance entails focus, endurance, and repetition.

Focus

We've covered focus pretty well already, but it is a vital part of this chapter's topic and therefore cannot be overlooked.

In 2009 Jan Koum founded WhatsApp Inc. The company was named after the mobile app he would soon create. Over the following months he spent countless hours writing code. Frustration brought him to the point of almost quitting at times, but WhatsApp eventually began to see significant growth in its user base. Over the next two years the app ranked in the top twenty of all apps in the United States. Koum's app was *hot*. Still, *Forbes* magazine journalist Parmy Olson reported that when asked why he was not pushing WhatsApp to the media like most people in his position would do, Koum replied, "Marketing and press kicks up dust, it gets in your eye, and then you're not focusing on the product."

Fast-forward three years, and Facebook acquires his app for an astounding *$19 billion*. The story of the huge acquisition flooded the media, and Koum became an instant celebrity (and billionaire). With that kind of money one would think that the company's headquarters would have a "WhatsApp" sign on it, marking its territory. You would, however, be wrong. Koum did not see it as necessary. In his eyes it would fulfill no purpose other than an ego boost, noted Olson. "We all know where we work." Jan Koum exemplifies the power of focus. "I want to do one thing, and do it well."

Endurance

My dad used to always joke that people try to child-proof things but end up adult-proofing them instead. "Like those containers. A child is going to figure it out. They're going to keep trying until they get it. . . . They've seen it open before so they know it can open again. If an adult can't figure it out, they'll give up out of frustration. In a child's mind, when they want to do something, nothing else in the world matters. They have all day!" Based on what I have seen myself over the years, I would not bet against my father's analysis.

Adults are "smart," so they quickly analyze tasks and decide the "best ways" to complete them. After exhausting all options that make sense to them, they begin to perceive that something is wrong (i.e., broken). Of course, if the container is broken there is no point of trying anymore. For this reason, adults are quicker to quit.

Children, on the other hand, do not rely on analysis as much as trial and error. They are more likely to open the container repeatedly, applying various angles and levels of pressure for however long it takes to open it. We often think, *How did that little kid figure that out? Kids are so smart.* In reality and more likely, they just refused to give up. They simply outlast their obstacle. It is not a matter of exhausting all of their options. It is only a matter of *time*—not "how" but "when." People face many pains and obstacles on their path to success, but time reigns as the most difficult opponent. It is uncompromising, relentless, and constant, which is why endurance is a key to success.

Repetition

In 1992 a man noticed that wool hats were becoming really popular in his neighborhood, but they were too expensive in his opinion. He decided to create his own version of the hats and asked his mother to teach him how to sew. On his first day of business, he sold eighty hats in no time. He knew he was on to something, and this minor success led Daymond John to create the clothing brand FUBU.

Initially, John began putting the FUBU logo on every type of apparel possible, and it began to catch fire. Capitalizing on each opportunity, he eventually made his way to a popular trade show where FUBU was able to get three hundred thousand dollars in orders. Without the funds to manufacture and fill the orders, his mother took out a second mortgage on their house and turned it into a factory. The decision allowed FUBU to get into more stores and continue to grow in popularity.

Daymond John continued to push the brand until, once again, FUBU was in dire need of money in order to expand. This time there was no house to mortgage. They needed a bank loan *badly*, and it did not come easily. John was denied a loan by twenty-seven banks before his mother put an ad in the newspaper. Then Samsung's textile division called. They struck a deal, and FUBU went on to revolutionize the fashion industry in the 1990s. Today the company has grossed over $6 billion in global sales.

Many people would not have made more than seven attempts to get funding, let alone twenty-seven. This is a testament to repetition. Pandora, the now popular website and mobile app, existed for ten years before becoming synonymous with online radio. Comedian Steve Harvey struggled with homelessness and was thirty-six years old before receiving his first big break, becoming the host of *Showtime at the Apollo*. J. K. Rowling's extremely popular *Harry Potter* book series was turned down by twelve publishers before getting a deal. Today, the series has made billions of dollars. Success takes time, effort, and commitment. Endure long enough and your efforts will certainly pay off.

"Life has a way of making sure you really want whatever it is you say you want...and if you don't really want it, it's gonna weed you out...if you really want it...it's just a matter of time before your hard work and passion are going to cut through all of it"

—*Miguel*

~ CHAPTER 14 ~

Mindset #4: Faith

"I think I can."—The Little Engine That Could

Emmitt Perry Jr. grew up in a poor, abusive home in New Orleans, Louisiana. In an attempt to separate himself from his physically and verbally abusive father, he changed his name to Tyler Perry at the age of sixteen. After watching *Oprah* he began writing a journal as a therapeutic release. Eventually, he decided to turn the stories in his journal into a play.

Perry moved to Atlanta with nothing but his car and his dream. He worked as a bill collector and car salesman, saving up twelve thousand dollars to rent a playhouse in 1992. After doing some promotion, Perry thought twelve hundred people would come for the weekend release. Only thirty came, all friends and family. "I knew every one of them," Perry said, "but I didn't stop."

From 1993 to 1997 Perry did the same thing, working all year to save up for one weekend, and he met with the same result each time. During this period he even lived in the streets when he could not make ends meet. In 1998 Perry finally felt overwhelmed. He already had not had much success before, but now the heat in the theatre was out on a cold day. He felt like giving up, and then a miracle happened. "I looked out the window [of the theater], and there was a line around the corner."

Today, Tyler Perry is well known throughout the United States. His plays became wildly popular, prompting historic runs in film and television. He has been featured in countless media outlets, including regular appearances on *Forbes* magazine's "Most Powerful" list.

Sometimes a person becomes self-accountable and takes charge in life—finds a focus, takes action, and perseveres through many setbacks—but *still* has yet to achieve success. Setbacks can be hard. As a matter of fact, they can be *extremely* hard.

Perry focused on one idea and persisted for seven years. Reflecting on where he had come from and as advice to others, he once stated, "You cannot control the sunshine, you cannot control the weather, and you cannot control what little locusts will come and try and destroy it. All you can do is plant your seed in the ground, water it, and believe."

Those words hold great truth. When you are genuinely doing everything in your power to ensure your success, all you can do is have faith that things will eventually line up in your favor. Otherwise, why continue?

The Container

Recall the "container" example used when discussing endurance in the chapter on perseverance. An interesting note is that, although the adult gave up quickly, this outcome could easily have been changed. Consider if you told someone that there was a *trick* to opening the container. They would not have assumed so quickly that it was broken and probably would have proceeded to try and figure it out. They may initially have become frustrated to the point of quitting. Still, knowing that there *is* in fact a way to open the container would have caused them to revisit the problem from time to time, hoping to see it from a different perspective.

Intellect alone can only do so much. When it comes to our obstacles, cracking the code is often only a matter of time. The more combinations you try, the more likely you are to be right. Often in life there is a trick to getting around our obstacles: *faith.*

Faith fuels patience. It is belief. If you do not believe you can do something, why would you try to do it? Even greater, why would you suffer pain and sacrifice attempting to reach a goal you do not even think you can achieve? Hopefully your answer is, "I wouldn't," because the converse would be absolutely insane.

Faith breeds perseverance. No man or woman has achieved greatly without first believing they could. No man or woman has ever achieved greatly without faith.

Let Nothing Go Unrealized
If I should die a broken man it'd be no fault of mine,
If I should fail over and over again it'd be only after I've tried,
Maybe I'm meant to be nothing at all but I'll never accept that in my mind,
One day I won't get up after I fall but I'll never quit fighting for time,
If I should die a broken man and my wants remain unfulfilled,
It'd be no fault of mine I live unbroken in faith and will
– Sean Taylor

Summary of The 4 Mindsets Achievement

1. **Put all your energy and focus** on achievement, not preventing failure.

2. **Self-accountability** means life is your fault.
   a. You have the power to change yourself and your life.
   b. *You* give your obstacles power, so don't.
   c. Obstacles are only opportunities to become better.
   d. Obstacles such as race, gender, class, and even disability should be looked at no differently than any other obstacle. When you hold yourself accountable, obstacles can be reduced to almost being inconsequential.

3. **Focus** breeds mastery.
   a. Put all of your eggs in one basket. If it breaks, get a new one.
   b. For most people, diversification should be a strategy of maintenance, not progress.
   c. Pay attention. You cannot buy time, but if you focus you will have more of it (and use it effectively).

4. **Perseverance** is a combination of focus, endurance, and repetition.
   a. There are many pains and obstacles that people face on their path to success, but time reigns as the most difficult opponent. It is uncompromising. It is relentless. It is constant.

5. **Faith** is your lifeline when you have done all that you can do. Without faith there is no reason to keep trying.
   a. It is only logical to stop trying to do something that you do not think is possible.

Core 3

Habit

~ CHAPTER 15 ~

The Power and Importance of Habit

Particularly when your goals are lofty, the secret is to persist on a certain thought process until it reaches the *habitual* scale. This realm is extremely powerful, where thoughts and actions integrate and align with instincts. Just as you get up and walk across the floor to turn the lights on in the morning without consciously telling yourself, *Get out of bed, take ten steps to the door, and flip the switch*, once you achieve this unconscious approach to a new habit, you've successfully adopted it.

The Power: Good vs Bad Habits

Do you remember the following highway traffic scenario from earlier in book?

On the Highway
A highway full of cars has a flow of traffic, but each individual has a destination in mind. If you have been driving for any length of time, at some point you have

probably experienced driving home and somewhere along the way slipping into "daydream mode." You may have missed a turn, ended up at the wrong place, or perhaps even made it home without vivid recollection of the previous few minutes and how you arrived there.

Two important outcomes of this scenario are (1) you end up at the wrong place and (2) you make it home, but have no recollection of how you arrived there after your last point of consciousness. In the latter situation, the correct destination was *still* achieved. How could this be? Habits, of course!

I once helped a friend move into a condo. When I asked her how things were coming along a few weeks later, she told me that one day after picking her daughter up from daycare, she drove to her old apartment, not noticing the error until she was at the gate. Her old "good" habit was now a bad one, and she had to rid herself of it.

Just as good habits consistently lead you in the right direction, bad habits lead you in the wrong one. Good and bad habits almost always have different destinations in mind, which is why good habits are so important. Good habits act as a personal insurance policy for times of absentmindedness. In situations when we face uncertainty or fail to focus adequately, good habits can carry us through to victory. Likewise, bad habits will bring on defeat if you do not acknowledge and change them. Think about it. How many times have you heard of a talented individual being undone by their inability to get rid of a bad habit?

The Importance: Ring the Alarm!!!
I try to work out or be active at least four days a week and have been doing so for some time. Every once in a while, though, usually during the holidays when visiting family, I break that habit. First it begins as *I'll just do it tomorrow. I have too much to do*

today. Then by the third missed day, my thoughts are adamantly urging me to get back on track. By the time a full week passes, my body is screaming, "Don't do this to me, man! I feel horrible!" and I feel progressively worse until I redeem myself.

My point? Once a habit is ingrained into your routine, you become very aware of breaking it. Your habits come with built-in alarms. This insurance is one of the many perks of good habits. No matter how developed your good habits are, wrong turns happen. What matters is your ability to be aware of them and then get back on course.

In the following chapters I present general approaches you should make into habits if you desire success. These good habits are fundamentals that can be tailored and applied to any goal. So many people never make it past the first step of making a Pure Choice. Taking action separates you from the majority. The right mindset helps overcome setbacks and the power of habit will propel you to the top. *Consciously* form good habits so that you can *unconsciously* move toward success.

"Develop the habits, you've got the brain power, you got the energy, but develop the habits of success." –Warren Buffett

CHAPTER 16

Good Habit #1: Maximize Efficiency

Analyze and be selective about your actions. Time is valuable, so use it wisely. Do not waste it on activities with low returns. Trivial pursuits are obvious instances that offer a low return on your time invested, but a less-talked-about inefficiency is the traditionally encouraged "hard work." Although honorable, working hard can rob an individual of one's life if done blindly.

Work Smart, Work Hard

When Jordan Belfort was twenty-three years old, he owned a business that sold meat and seafood door-to-door. Driven to become rich, he wanted to expand his footprint as quickly as possible. His operation grew fast and looked promising, but by the age of twenty-five Belfort found himself filing for bankruptcy. He ended up working for a brokerage firm and took a liking to the industry. Seeing opportunity, he eventually opened his own firm and found himself a millionaire by the age of twenty-eight.

If you are familiar with Belfort's story you know that he participated in a variety of illegal activities, leading to the loss of his company and twenty-two months in jail for securities fraud and money laundering. Despite these unfortunate flaws in judgment, he later reflected on an extremely important lesson. Belfort observed that he had not put in anywhere near as much work in the world of stocks as he had during his days pushing meat and seafood. Speaking of the food business he said, "I was pretty talented . . . but the margins were too small." Stocks, however, made him a lot of money, even before breaking the law.

"Work hard" is incomplete advice that leads many people to work ambitiously at something that will never return the value of their efforts. Instead, what people should do is *work hard at working smart*. Whatever actions you plan to take, make sure they actually have the ability to produce the result you hope to receive. Working smart is not necessarily about the *easiest* route but the one with the highest return relative to the amount of time expended.

For example, if you want to improve your standardized test scores, you do not simply take the test again and again. You must know the different subject areas and then study the relevant content within each of those areas. From another perspective, basketball players do not improve *best* by simply playing in game situations all of the time. They get a far higher return working on specific moves and shot mechanics. A person who targets the right areas can achieve the same result or greater in a fraction of the time than a person who does not.

In football, technique is stressed so that players get a desired result while minimizing stress to the body. Simple machines such as ramps and pulleys allow people to move objects while using far less energy. In business, this same concept leads to the automation of processes that are simple but time consuming.

Successful people ensure that they get the best return on value for their time. They are always on the lookout for more efficient methods. Keep efficiency in mind when you are trying to increase your competency to attain a goal. *Good* practices are not *best* practices. If there is a low ceiling, no matter how much work you put in, you will only be able to go so high. Success does not come from working hard for the sake of it but from working smart for the sake of ensuring that your hard work does not go in vain. Be smart enough to work hard at the right things. Cater your choice of habits to focus on what will give you a better return in value for whatever you want in life.

Do not be fooled into thinking that *productive* and *efficient* are the same thing. Blindly working hard is like doing leg workouts until you can jump higher when there is a ladder right next to you. Your first-known "good options" are not always your best ones. Everyone has to start somewhere, but do not stop looking for a better way.

As Belfort found out, "If your business model is wrong . . . you can work twenty-two hours a day and you won't make a dime."

CHAPTER 17

Good Habit #2: Immersion

What is your mental diet? Everybody has the choice to nurture their mind or leave it malnourished. Just as the human body displays internal health through skin and weight, people's lives are merely broadcasts of their mental health. Fortunately, people can alter their thinking habits just like changing their diet.

To reinforce the information in this book, you should review it as much as possible. Think daily about the powers of success. Now that you know them, you will notice affirmations of these truths everywhere. Also, you should regularly look for speeches, books, videos, events, people, and activities that inspire you to succeed. Use any helpful source. Particularly if you have bad thoughts and habits, you must brainwash yourself for success. Feed your mind at least as often as your body.

Speeches are especially great sources for daily intake because you can do other things while you listen to them. There are plenty on the Internet. Find a short one that *really* inspires you to chase your goals relentlessly and listen to it every day for two weeks.

Twice a day is recommended for the first two-week period—once when you wake up and once before bed. Then find another speech.

Do this repeatedly while making use of other sources of inspiration as well. The world is constantly hitting you with things to derail you, so you need to reinforce your thoughts. It is a 100 percent guarantee that the world will bombard you with distraction and discouragement, but the same is not so for positivity and encouragement. The images and conversations that people encounter each day often slash and burn through their good thoughts, leaving them barren and unfit for growth. For this reason you must actively cultivate your own garden. Plant your own seeds. This is your defense mechanism, your pesticide, and your foundation.

You need to habitually feed yourself specific Pure Choice information as well. Get in the right environment and observe. A dancer not only dances but studies other dancers, too. Filmmakers study film, actors study acting technique, and so on. Becoming great at something is more than simply *doing*. Make use of the experiences and perspectives of others who are in your line of work. You do this through study.

Set aside at least thirty minutes each day to read about your industry or practice. Study the past and keep up with current events. Hang around people who talk about topics complimentary to your goal. Find a website related to your interest and set it as your Internet browser's homepage. Make it as easy as possible on yourself to come across good information and ideas. If you are lucky, a radio or TV show may even cover topics specific to your Pure Choice.

Wrap your mind fully around what you choose to accomplish. Make it a part of who you are. Your search for information should be so much of a habit that you begin to come across beneficial input without conscious pursuit. *Feed your mind* and immerse yourself in whatever you choose to achieve.

CHAPTER 18

Good Habit #3: Create Deliverables

The idea is simple. Break big goals into smaller tasks. When you make this practice a habit, intimidating goals will no longer exist in your life. In the world of business, the term *deliverable* is a product of this concept. Your grand vision should work as guidance as you complete the smaller tasks—deliverables— required to get there.

Will Smith has cited this concept as helping him when he competes with other people. He learned this lesson as a kid when his father had him and his brother build a new brick wall on the side of his shop. He recalled thinking, *There's going to be a hole here forever!* However, a year and a half later, Smith and his brother had completed the hefty task. In an interview on *The Charlie Rose Show*, Smith intellectualized his experience:

> "You don't try and build a wall. You don't set out to build a wall. You don't say I'm going

to build the biggest, baddest, greatest wall that's ever been built. You don't start there...You say, 'I'm going to lay this brick as perfectly as a brick can be laid. There will not be one brick on the face of the earth that will be laid better than this brick that I'm going to lay in this next 10 minutes...and you do that every single day...and soon you have a wall.'"

People are often paralyzed by a task's enormity. Breaking a goal down into smaller steps is not only less intimidating psychologically but the only rational way to reach most goals. The number of steps into which a task can be broken down naturally relates to its size. A simple approach that usually works is to identify a beginning, middle, and an end, and then distinguish definitive steps within each. After that, you can break down each step into however many smaller steps will help you complete the task. For example, this book can be broken down into three sections, and the parts and chapters within each section can be considered individual steps (which could be further broken down).

What is important is making sure that each step you write down is *clear and concrete*. Clarity makes the steps easier to communicate to others, if necessary, while also lessening the likelihood of forgetting or misinterpreting your own words later in the process. Additionally, if you are not concrete, you are working inefficiently. Executing ambiguity is incredibly difficult.

Student: "How do you get to Mount Olympus?"
Aristotle: "By simply ensuring that each step you take is toward Mount Olympus."

CHAPTER 19

Good Habit #4: Prepare

Getting out of the car, I closed the door and looked at my reflection in the window. My tie was crooked. I took a deep breath and slowly released air as I straightened the navy blue fabric until the knot was in perfect symmetry with my dress shirt. *I guess this is what it feels like to be a grown-up*, I thought. I was sixteen years old and ten minutes away from my first job interview.

At 9:30 a.m. I shook hands with Britney. After our greetings she told me that someone would be joining us and led me to a table outside of the retail store where two women and a man sat in conversation. *Aw, man! This is crazy!* I stood there shaking everyone's hands in complete shock. I was nervous enough about the interview already, and now I had an audience. As I sat down I contemplated the pain to come. *I didn't know what I was going to say to one person, but four?* I thought to myself.

When the trainee asked her first question I answered calmly and articulately. *That wasn't so bad*, I reasoned with myself. As the questions kept rolling, I kept answering. It felt as if everything rolled off my tongue smoothly—so much so that, following one of my answers, I thought, *That was genius! I can't believe you said that!* This went on for about twenty minutes before we all rose from our chairs and parted ways. On my walk back to the car with a big smile on my face I sighed in relief. Wow! Everything my family taught me just . . . came out. . . . Everything I learned from Mom, Dad, my uncle, Grandpa . . . *everybody*!"

* * * * *

Years ago I read a book about Michael Jordan in which he addressed a question on nervousness when faced with the opportunity of taking the game-winning shot. I cannot recall the statement verbatim, but he said something along the lines of, "In that moment I am not nervous because I work hard. I know I have done everything possible to get me ready for that moment. At that point it is out of my hands, and I am not nervous because I know I am prepared." Preparation is key; Michael Jordan was well known for working harder than anyone, even *after* being considered the best basketball player in the world.

At my first job interview I was prepared without even knowing it. As intimidating as the interview was, all of the annoyingly persistent critique my family members had given me my entire life was so ingrained in my subconscious that I did not have to draw upon it purposely. All of my family's quizzing on my goals and insisting to speak proper English, among other things, gave me the communication skills necessary to ace my interview.

My words came out effortlessly when the time called for them. I only needed to acquire the skills so that when the moment arrived, my instincts could take the driver's seat. My family made sure I had these skills before I could even appreciate their significance. This experience marked the first time I could truly comprehend the benefit of preparation. When you are prepared, why be nervous? You can do nothing else when you have done all you can.

Preparation and Instinct: Maximizing Performance
Varying definitions are available for "instinct," but *Merriam-Webster's* dictionary offers the best one, in my opinion: "a natural or inherent aptitude, impulse, or capacity; a largely inheritable and unalterable tendency of an organism to make a complex and specific response to environmental stimuli without involving reason."

Contrary to many people's beliefs, instincts are not fixed. A common misconception is that instincts are complete at birth and "unalterable," as the definition states. Some say, "What you are born with, you live with," but you can train your instincts. Instincts grow and develop just as you do. Although people are born with the most basic of instincts, over time their instincts are molded by individual encounters, societal influences, and the choices they make.

Playing Catch: Fool Me Once
When I was younger, a friend and I always argued about who could catch better. As a result, whenever we had something to throw, we played catch, usually trying to catch the other off guard to increase the chance of the other dropping the object. One day I decided to play a prank on my friend. I colored an orange with a black marker on one side, calling his attention after I already threw the orange to him. Just as I expected, he caught it. He smiled proudly at his athletic prowess. I smiled back, pointing at his hands, which were covered in black marker.

A few weeks later I happened to have an orange again, and as usual I tried to catch him off guard, launching the orange into the air and only calling his name after it was well on its way to his corner of the room. He looked up and immediately dodged the orange. As I looked at him, perplexed by his reaction, he taunted, "You're not going to get me with that one again!" I thought about it and burst out laughing. I had completely forgotten about the prank I pulled three weeks earlier. There was no marker on the orange.

Every experience you have is added to your mind, and your instincts use them all. Knowing the game we play, my friend's instincts sent his body into motion in order to catch the orange the first time around. The second time his instincts quickly analyzed that an orange was in the air, that I was the one who threw it, and what happened the last time I performed that act. Consequently, instead of the usual catch, his instincts screamed, "Abort mission!" and demanded that he duck.

After something is learned, your instincts have a new option to consider when the time for quick action arises. Moreover, after you practice something repeatedly, your instincts can execute for you that much better. *Your instincts become smarter as you become smarter.* Why? Because both are drawing from the same well.

Instincts are often steps ahead of what can be accomplished without their assistance. They are a seemingly superhuman element of mankind. Conscious minds cannot process information nearly as fast. No one can describe this phenomenon better than an athlete. For the most part, the pace is too fast during a game for athletes to consciously control all of their actions. Athletes are generally bound to their instincts, but every skill they practice is available as needed.

Many athletes even go as far as declaring they play *better* when they do not think. This is because humans' ability to evaluate the present, past, and future can become a hindrance and weaken action by allowing one of the mindsets of failure to take charge.

One day, a friend of mine who played football made an interesting observation: "You know, it's crazy, because for the most part I feel unstoppable on the field but in the moments I stop and go, *Whoa, he's pretty big*, or *He's fast*, then I'm finished. I'm probably going to get run over or miss the tackle. . . . You can't think about it, man."

A split second of hesitation has the power to harm. Professional basketball player Kobe Bryant also alludes to how the conscious mind can be a hindrance when describing the Zone. *The Zone* is a term often used in sports to describe a state when instinct takes over completely and you feel invincible.

> "When you get in that zone it's just that supreme confidence it's going in [the basket]... it's not a matter of this or that...it's going in...Everything slows down. You just have supreme confidence. But when that happens you really try not to focus on what's going on, because you can lose it in a second...You have to really try to, you know...stay in the present and not let anything break that rhythm."

As noted earlier in this book, fear and doubt are distractions that may come into play when processing an obstacle ahead. If you allow them to seep in, the resulting hesitation weakens your actions. Instincts are incredible judges of circumstances, only minimally, if at all, affected by the noise of the conscious mind. While in the Zone, an individual must completely surrender to instinct. Bryant shows that he realizes this need when he speaks of trying to "stay in the present."

Your intuition is smarter than you are when a quick decision is necessary. It considers more information in a shorter time. The mind can operate at this speed when not distracted by conscious thought. People's instincts are usually more powerful than their conscious mind, largely because of their boldness as compared to weak, cautious, thought-out action.

The only reservation in regard to instinct should be realizing the difference between instinct and desire. Is your gut saying do it, or do you just *want* to do it? This question can be extremely tricky. Instead, do not focus on distinguishing the two but simply on empowering your instincts through preparation. You can also practice tuning into your instincts by listening to them in small, low-risk circumstances and slowly building trust in them from there. The more they are exposed and the easier it is for you to submit to them, the more accurate your instincts will be when they take over.

Whether you have a speech to give, an interview to prepare for, a potential account you are closing on, or any other goal, study all you can then allow your instincts to take over when the time is right. Instincts take whatever you do to another level, but they can only work with what you give them, which is why preparation is important.

"I have begun to listen to the teaching my blood whispers to me."

–Hermann Hesse

Summary of Core 3: Habit

1. **Habit** is discipline; discipline is habit. There is no need to draw upon willpower when you possess the habits of success.
    a. Good habits act as a personal insurance policy. Even when you are not aware, they will carry you to victory.
    b. Bad habits will lead you to defeat.

2. **Maximize efficiency** to make the best use of your time and the most out of your efforts.
    a. Success does not come from working hard for the sake of it, but from working smart for the sake of ensuring that your hard work does not go in vain.
    b. Always keep your eyes open for a better way to do what you need to be done.

3. **Immerse** yourself in the behaviors, environments, and mindsets necessary for your success.
    a. Find something that inspires you and revisit it on a daily basis to embed the message deep within your subconscious.
    b. Immerse yourself in the fundamentals for success (your foundation) as well as the things necessary to succeed at your specific goal.

4. **Create and execute deliverables** to accomplish big tasks.
    a. People are often paralyzed by the enormity of a task. Breaking a goal down into smaller steps is not only less psychologically intimidating but the only way to actually reach the goal.
    b. Create clear and concrete steps to take you where you want to go.

5. **Preparation** breeds confidence and minimizes the doubts that hinder performance.
    a. Your instincts are not fixed. They grow with you, drawing upon your well of experience.
    b. If you have done everything you can do, you can do nothing else but go for it.
    c. Learn how to hone your instincts.

Core Reinforcement

Keep This In Mind

CHAPTER 20

Mental Conditioning

"If I woke up tomorrow and my industry no longer existed, I'd pick something else...anything...and whatever I do I'm going to succeed." —Karl Route

"Wait! What if I waste my time chasing success at something I later find out not to be my passion?"

This question represents a common, fear-driven reason for not making a commitment. It is, in fact, a reasonable concern, but be assured that *it does not matter*

Consider something Steve Harvey voiced in the speech referenced earlier in this book. When addressing the reason people reach various levels of success, he essentially boiled it down to *mental conditioning*. Harvey suggested that an individual's mind must be trained to perform at the level in life at which that person would like to be. You should become well-acclimated to the persistence, level of effort, and overall outlook your perceived success requires.

To be successful, condition yourself for success. When the personal philosophies and habits of successful people in different fields are dissected, their cores are found to be rather similar. Doctors, lawyers, politicians, actors, musicians, athletes, and those in the business world might need distinctive skills to perform in their respective fields, but performing at a high level in *anything* means using the *3 Core Powers of Success*. Furthermore, the mentalities and habits I describe in this book not only lead to mastering the 3 Core Powers but can then be applied to honing the aforementioned skills in specific fields as well.

The Terminator

A great example of conditioning for success is Arnold Schwarzenegger. As a teenager living in Austria, he dreamed he would one day travel to America and become "Mr. Universe," the name awarded to the winner of the International Federation of Bodybuilding competition. Unfortunately, everyone saw the young Arnold as a fool. His friends made fun of him, and his father was ashamed, sending Arnold to the military to put him on the right path. Arnold's goal was in jeopardy.

A strict daily routine in the military took most of his time and energy, but even worse, his military base had no weight sets. To compensate, Schwarzenegger rigged up anything he could find into makeshift workout equipment. When everyone else went to sleep, he stayed up an extra three hours to work out, and he woke up early to do the same thing in the morning. When he was invited to an amateur competition in Stuttgart, Germany, he was excited, except for one issue: he was not allowed to leave the base during basic training. After much contemplation, he made a Pure Choice; he would go regardless of the consequences. In dramatic fashion, Schwarzenegger won his first competition.

Schwarzenegger's leave infuriated his officers, and he served solitary confinement upon his return. Still, he eventually gained their support. The officers built him a weight set and even allowed him extra food to put on muscle mass. When Schwarzenegger finally made his way to America, he won the title he had dreamed of for so long: Mr. Universe. This is merely an abridged account of Schwarzenegger's journey, but be assured that his quest to achieve his Pure Choice conditioned his mind for success.

After winning Mr. Universe and going on to win Mr. Olympia seven times, Schwarzenegger changed his focus. The bodybuilder decided he wanted to be the biggest movie star in America, despite his near-incomprehensible English. Still, he became a household name, with his movies grossing billions of dollars over his career. Meanwhile, he married into the Kennedy family, practically U.S. royalty. Possibly even more amazing, the movie star later decided he wanted to run for governor of California, one of the highest-profile states in America. He even ran on the Republican ballot, despite the Kennedys being Democratic icons. Of course, it is not surprising that he won.

Schwarzenegger let no obstacle or opinion stop him. Not even the family he married into or his own father could dictate his decisions. His goals were his and his alone.

If you exercise Pure Choice and embark on the journey of conditioning necessary to succeed, you have, in a sense, already won. If you happen to realize that something else is your passion, you will possess the fundamentals necessary to succeed in that field as well. You will have already acquired best practices of success and be on a fast track of sorts. Conversely, if you still have not conditioned your mind, achieving success in your passion will be harder. For this reason, if you do not yet know your passion, *just pick something* to master and begin to condition yourself. Make a Pure Choice, acquire the mindsets, and develop the right habits. When an individual masters the 3 Core Powers of Success, *any* goal can be achieved.

~ CHAPTER 21 ~

The 3 Cores: Bringing It All Together

To understand how the 3 Core Powers work together, you need a basic understanding of how the Earth works. To begin, here is a simplified version of how science today understands the Earth:

Beginning from the center, Earth's layers are the inner core, the outer core, the mantle, and the crust. The inner core is made of solid iron. The outer core is made of rocky material that has been heated into a liquid state. The mantle is a cooler, less liquid version of the outer core. Finally, around the mantle is the crust, Earth's rocky outermost layer.

The most important part of this analogy lies in a process called *convection* (illustrated by the arrows in the figure), in which heat causes the fluids of the layers to rise and fall in a circular pattern. As the liquid moves in the path of the arrows, material is exchanged between each layer. Ultimately, the liquid escapes the mantle as semi-molten rock called *magma* and cools on the surface of the Earth, creating the crust. On this layer exists nature as we see it.

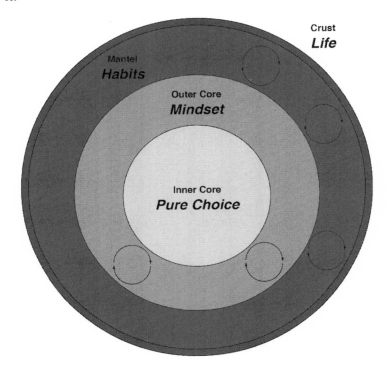

In considering the 3 Core Powers of Success, Pure Choice is the inner core, mindset is the outer core, and habit is the mantle. The surrounding crust is our life as we see it. Just as Earth's crust is a result of the inner material rising and hardening on the surface, a person's life is one's inner composition hardened externally. Essentially, it is a physical realization of how people exercise the 3 Core Powers. Each of the powers are constantly interacting through a convection-like process, slowly becoming more tangible. The choices you make, thoughts you have, and actions you take come together to determine your life as you know it.

Potential for Impact

As humans our need to reach our full potential is innate. Happiness is achieved when we use our potential to progress. True peace is found when we have used our talents fully and all potential has been exhausted. The world desperately needs more people to do so. More people to use the gifts they were given. More people to help others do the same.

The people who have done so in the past have made a great impact on society. We all have the power to create not just a better life for ourselves but a better world as a whole. After all, we are gODs.

Within every human is great potential. When we tap into this potential the feats we can perform are boundless. The 3 Core Powers of Success allow a person to effectively focus and direct their potential at a cause. As the cores are developed, they should be used to empower others. The cores are not meant to be squandered on one individual. They should be shared for all to benefit. When we seek to bring out the best in others just as much as we do for ourselves, we find ourselves having accomplished more than we ever could have imagined.

"I firmly believe that any man's finest hour, the greatest fulfillment of all that he holds dear, is that moment when he has worked his heart out on a good cause and he lies exhausted on the field of battle, victorious."
~Vince Lombardi

Appendix A
3 Core Evaluation

Pure Choice
1. Have you made a Pure Choice?

2. If not, what factors are preventing you from making a Pure Choice? Are you worrying about external noise (friends, family, society)? Or internal noise (fear, lack of confidence, etc.)?

3. Is there any situation in your life that you do not want to be in but feel trapped? If so, know that you are not trapped and make a Pure Choice.

Consider each Pure Choice as a goal. Use the following questions to examine each individual goal.

Mindset (Mental Foundation)
1. How much time do you dedicate each week to developing your mind for success? Each day? (Consider inspirational readings or lectures, disciplinary techniques, mental exercises, thinking habits, etc.)

2. How often do you self-reflect?

3. What are the areas in which you fall short and may need some help to complete your task?

4. Do you have long-term goals and desires?

Mindset: (Obstacle approach)

1. What are your priorities?

2. What are the biggest obstacles you face in achieving your goals?

3. Do you spend too much time focusing on obstacles?

4. What abilities must you acquire to overcome your obstacles and achieve your goals? (*This is where your focus should be!*)

Habits (Action into success)

1. Identify the steps that will get you to your goal.

2. What are the primary habits that will propel you into success in achieving those steps and, ultimately, your goal?

3. How much time do you dedicate each day to achieving your goals according to your plan?

Note: The more choices you are pursuing, the less effective these methods and your efforts will be. Obviously one Pure Choice is ideal, but if you must have multiple ones it is recommended that Appendix B is considered.

Appendix B

The Timeline

Although nothing beats having a singular focus, a great method can help you achieve several goals with a similar level of concentration: the timeline. You cannot do everything at once if you want to do anything well. The function of the timeline is to take multiple goals and arrange them where you can focus on each one as singularly as possible. At its best, goals will be arranged in an order that will build momentum. Each goal reached will empower you to complete the next goal more easily.

Goal 1: High School → Goal 2: College → Goal 3: Profession

In the basic example above, you can see how each goal prepares you for the next. The problem with this example is that most goals do not explicitly order themselves for you as this one does.

A friend of mine expressed that he had several goals but did not know where to start. He had twelve goals written down, so I immediately recommended he prioritize his list down to the most important few.

With that accomplished, I noticed that none of his goals had a specific date by which they needed to be started or finished. He wanted to write two books and start a business (completely unrelated to the books). However, like many people, he did not want to risk everything suddenly to pursue his undeveloped goals 24/7, which was fine. Still, we decided that it would not be smart to pursue his business idea half-heartedly. On the other hand, he could easily write his books in his spare time if he made the commitment, but which book would be first?

Of the two books, his hopes for one far exceeded the other.

With that noted, we came to the following conclusion after much discussion. First he would write book A, the less ambitious book. If done successfully, he would befriend key individuals and gain knowledge along the way that would improve the chances for success of the second book. Although the subject matter of the books was different, he knew that the people he wanted to contribute to his first book had friends who could help with his second book. Even better, some of their friends were in the industry of his business idea as well.

Second, he would leverage the momentum from his first book to aid the efforts in publishing his second one. This step could further his relationships in circles relevant to his goals and maybe even give him a little income. On top of that, books are businesses in their own right. He had never started a business before, and the books could be a training ground. Hopefully, by then, he would have a strong enough foundation to confidently quit his job and pursue his business. We also agreed that even if he were unable to leave work totally while building his business, he at least needed to get a job that would allow him more free time to scratch his entrepreneurial itch.

Of course, things may or may not work out how we plan. Still, this logical breakdown is a great way to attack multiple goals at once in a way that more closely mimics focusing on one thing at a time. The journey has not been without setback for my friend, but the last time I spoke to him, he was well on his way to goal number three.

The Idea Simplified
1. Identify your highest priorities.

2. Structure the order to achieve them (as much as you can) in a way that each goal empowers the next.

3. Create a reasonable deadline for accomplishing each goal.

Note: Some goals may concern an event with a deadline you cannot alter (e.g., "Win next year's marathon," "Increase profits this quarter," etc.), but with a little thought, this methodology can still be adapted and used within time constraints.

Appendix C

Applying Focus

Live Like A Genius

The more detail you process, the more time you seem to have and the more you spend that time wisely. Details are the key to preventing life from pushing you around. Focusing on these details is the tool best equipped to help you push back. Although new people, subjects, and other novel experiences organically increase focus, when it comes to combating familiarity to get the most out of your daily routine, try this approach:

1. Isolate a time to focus on a specific task (studying, cleaning, working out, etc.).

2. Remove all distractions from the work environment. If possible, switch environments every once in a while, even if that means simply moving to a different room in your house.

3. Divide lengthy tasks into shorter periods, two to three hours *at the most* per period.

4. Work solely on the intended task for length of a period. Immerse yourself and your thoughts fully into the given task.

5. Take a short break after each period to give your mind a rest.

6. Repeat steps 4 and 5 until the task is complete, or at a desired stopping point.

If you are wondering why you should divide long tasks into smaller intervals, it is because our focus tends to waver over extended periods of time. For this reason, time management methods such as the Pomodoro Technique suggest that work should be broken down into shorter intervals. Focus is mentally fatiguing, and focusing for too long eventually diminishes your returned value to the point of inefficiency. Still, going all in for short periods allows us to absorb more detail per minute.

Have you ever had a day where you had to fulfill several non-routine tasks, one at a time in different places, and by the time the day was over, the things you did earlier that morning felt like a completely different day altogether? It felt as if you accomplished a lot, and you probably did. This is the experience of having varying tasks short and submerging enough to allow intervals of deep focus. Shorts spurts of focus lengthen time from a relative standpoint of productivity. You perform at an increased efficiency per second. Try the aforementioned method. You will be surprised at how much more you got done in what felt to be a longer time than it actually was.

Acknowledgements

I would like to thank my family—including the Callaways. I work hard to make you proud and keep you all in mind more than you could ever know.

Thank you to the many other people who have contributed to my development. I have both observed and inquired, learning from your steps and missteps. As a matter of fact, the most relevant part of my learning has always come from quiet observance. For this reason, many of you do not know your impact on me and would be surprised to know that this message is addressed to you.

To maintain individuals' privacy I forgo providing names here, but I will be sure to make my gratitude known to all who would have been listed.

There are few gifts more thoughtful than a book. If you find this book to be beneficial, share it with someone. Good information is one of the most valuable gifts that can be given. Share the knowledge, share the love!

Visit youaregodinfo.com to read the author's blog, join the conversation and share ideas with other success-minded individuals.

Made in the USA
Middletown, DE
10 March 2022

62459442R00066